H THE O UR

WASP

JAY SHEETS

ILLUSTRATED BY
ROBYN LEIGH LEAR

Publisher's Cataloging-in-Publication Data

Sheets, Jay.
    The hour wasp / written by Jay Sheets / illustrated by Robyn Leigh Lear
    ISBN: 978-0-9882061-3-7

1. Poetry: General 2. Poetry: American - General I. Title
II. Author III. Illustrator

[accolades for jay sheets]

"If poetry is religion, *The Hour Wasp* is a sanctuary; a temple
in which Sheets guides us to the altar. He gives us room enough
to worship, seek absolution, or call forth ecstatic visions.
Throughout he tries on the cloak of monk, prophet, and shaman,
before settling effortlessly into the mantle of modern mystic.
All of this feels as deliberate as the intricacies of each work…
The Hour Wasp and what I will call its three phases because each
one permeates the other – casts us in shadow, gibbous ray, then
maximum incandescence." – Claudine Cain, *Black Elephant Lit*

"Like reading through a dream." – Ryann Crofoot

"I felt alive with every word, every sentence that I read.
Mesmerising, lyrical poetry accompanied by beautiful artwork…
This book is bursting, with emotions intertwined in creativity,
at the seams. Raw, original, sophisticated, and yet the poetry
rings with such candour. The writing style seems like that
of the Romantic poets and offers a magical escape, a surreal
transportation to our imaginations." – Shelley D.

"Ethereal, has a life-altering impact." – Korynne Michele

"The author, Jay Sheets, is an amalgam of abstraction and the
metaphysical. It is as if Whitman, Eliot, and Carlos Williams all
had a say in the thematic delivery of the work. Heavy abstraction,
crisp metaphors, vivid imagery, and personification littered
the collection, showing off the author's literary knowledge
and prowess. I learned as I read." – Joshua Dale, Thirty West
Publishing House

"This collection reads like the description of a dream in free verse.
It's almost as if someone tried to make poetry out of a surrealist
painting." –Andreea Martin, *Infinite Text Journal*

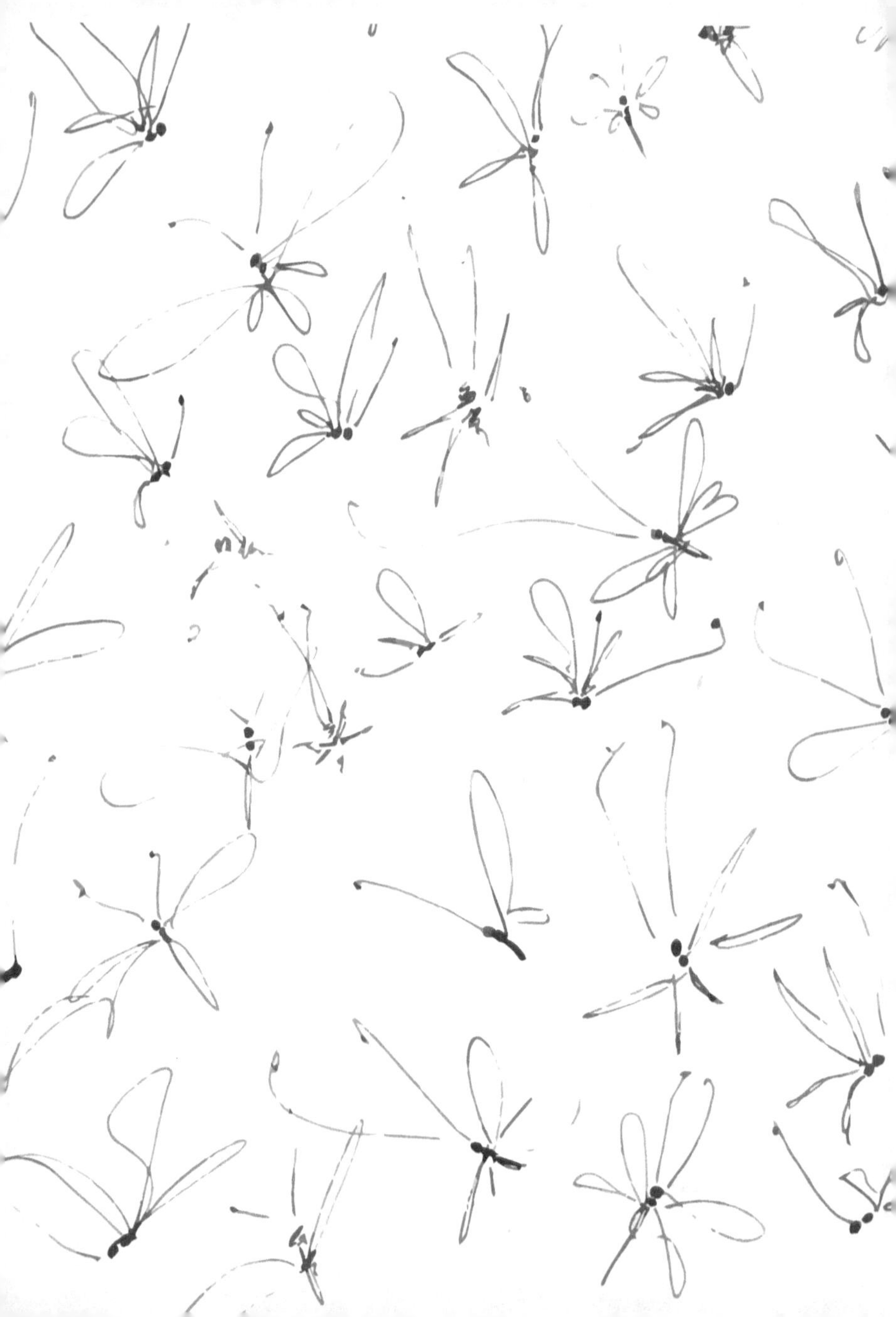

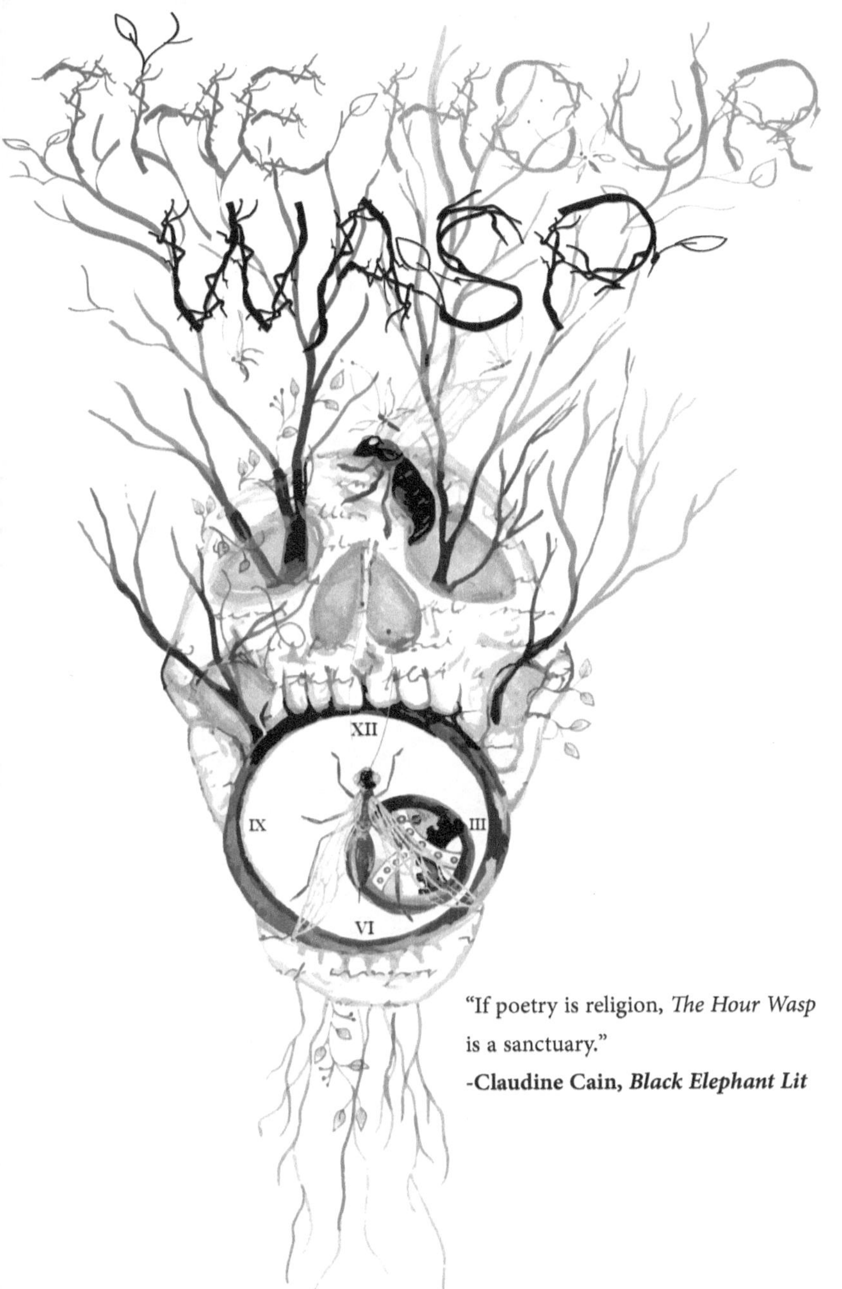

"If poetry is religion, *The Hour Wasp*
is a sanctuary."
-**Claudine Cain,** *Black Elephant Lit*

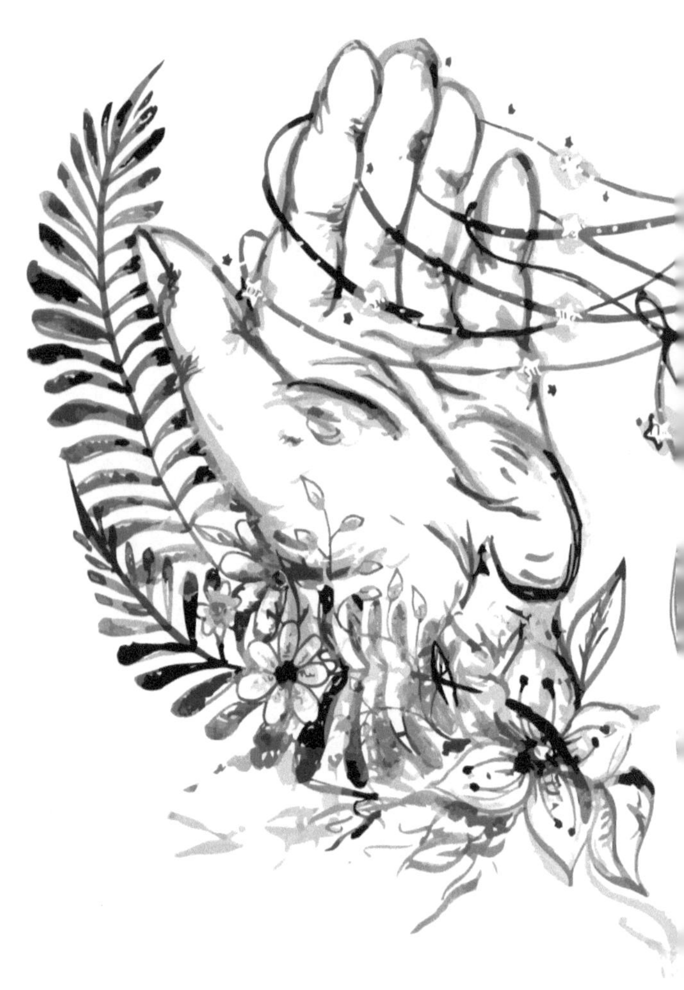

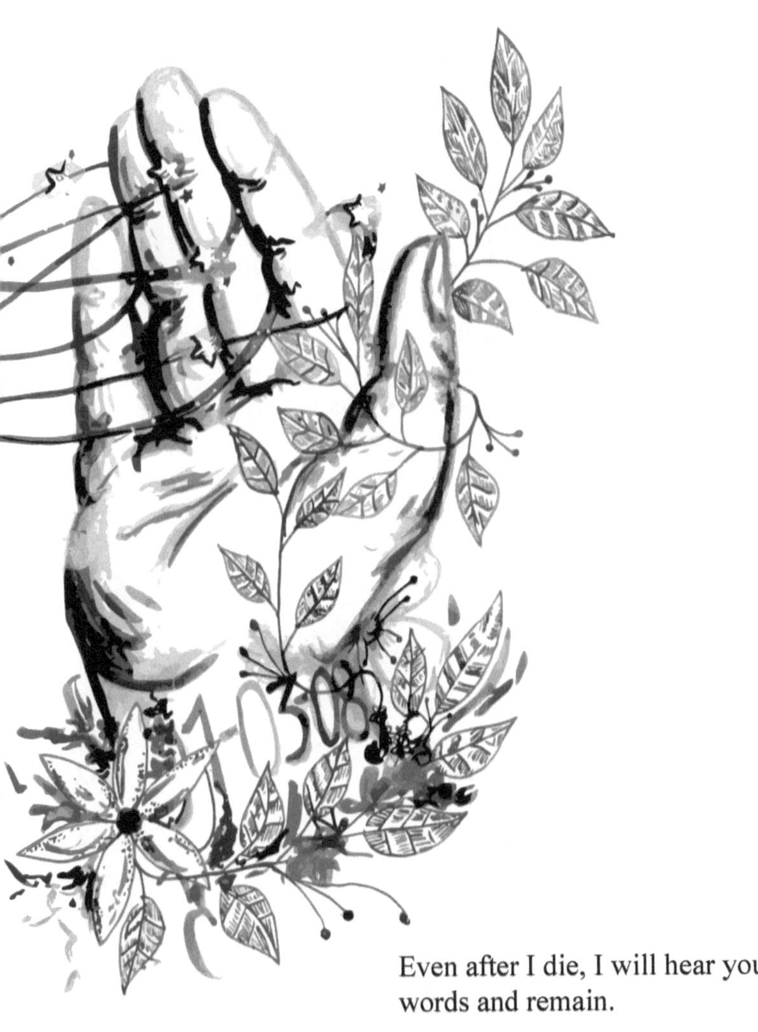

Even after I die, I will hear your words and remain.

Rubén Darío

[contents]

I

II

III

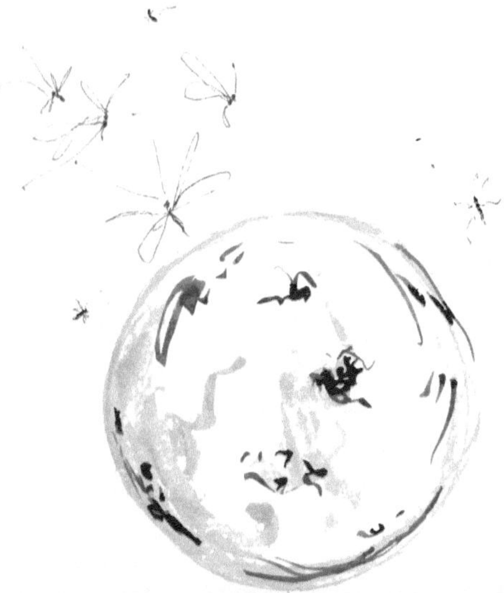

[foreword]

by Lance Umenhofer,
Author of *And the Soft Wind Blows*

In his debut collection, Jay Sheets remarkably sets out
to demonstrate to the world a simple adage, hope for the
hopeless. Immediately the tone is set and the reader finds
herself shrouded in a place, maybe a mind or ideology, by
dark, morose images, or dreams, with something residing in
those images that makes her want to delve deeper into what
they may mean for her, for those she's close to, for all of
humanity.

And it's this sense of waiting for the big reveal, the time
and place where life just doesn't seem so insurmountable,
because what, after all, are dreams that do not display hope
for the ones who dream them? Are we not all sometimes
stuck wading through the drab or dreary, searching with
every inkling of our inner selves, our passionate selves, for
even just the most minute ray of light to shine through and
illuminate the world for us?

The fact is, we're all waiting on that day, most of us still
waiting, and this collection serves to be a guidebook for those
times in the dark, for those times the great world might decide
to leave us behind, to drop us off in the void and carry on
ahead without us, those times in which we are dead weight,
for the world does not make time for us to get it together; no,
the world stops for no one, and it is my assertion that poetry
collections like these, when read with the heart, will help
their readers fight off that inevitable down-weigh of this great
world, used as shields, or protectors, to show the world that

yes, it still means something, despite that it may be trying to say otherwise.

For what Jay Sheets accomplishes in this collection is nothing short of a prodigy, a God-send, a new star born amid the deep, lifeless troughs of a black hole. The speaker, the poet, in the dark and damaged world, the world which affixes the mind on these sceneries and feelings, does what only the poet can do, write them down and dissolve them eternally.

This is a collection which should remain by the bedside table, one that only reveals all of its truth through time, through careful re-readings and longer bouts of time turning these poems over and over in one's mind; this is a collection that, despite the great, damaged world, illuminates itself and serves as a candle through the shadows, for the long, dire road ahead for all of us requires as much truth and as much light to be revealed so that we may take it on, shoulders lowered and mind affixed, and ready, for what is next.

And I hope that you and I, reader, can share the same, or similar, candle in the dark days to come. And may we hold steady and be ready with this (and I hope other) minute rays of light.

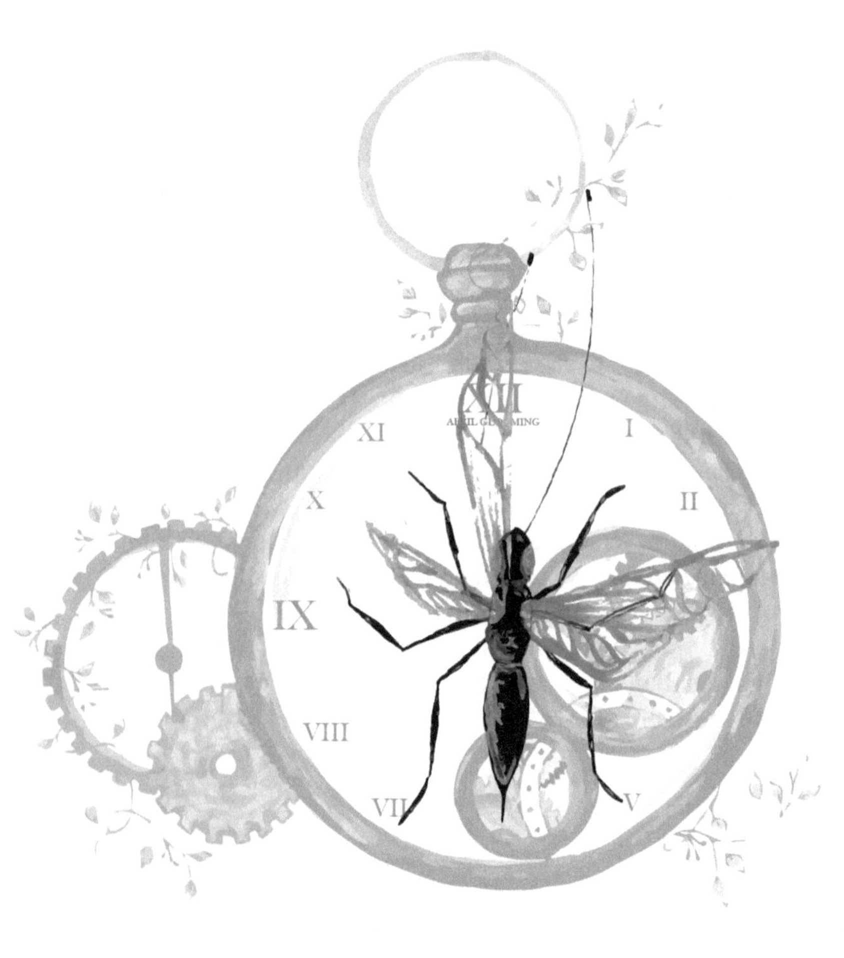

XI
X
IX
VIII
VII
XII
APRIL GLOAMING
I
II
V

I

[o the dark places we will go]

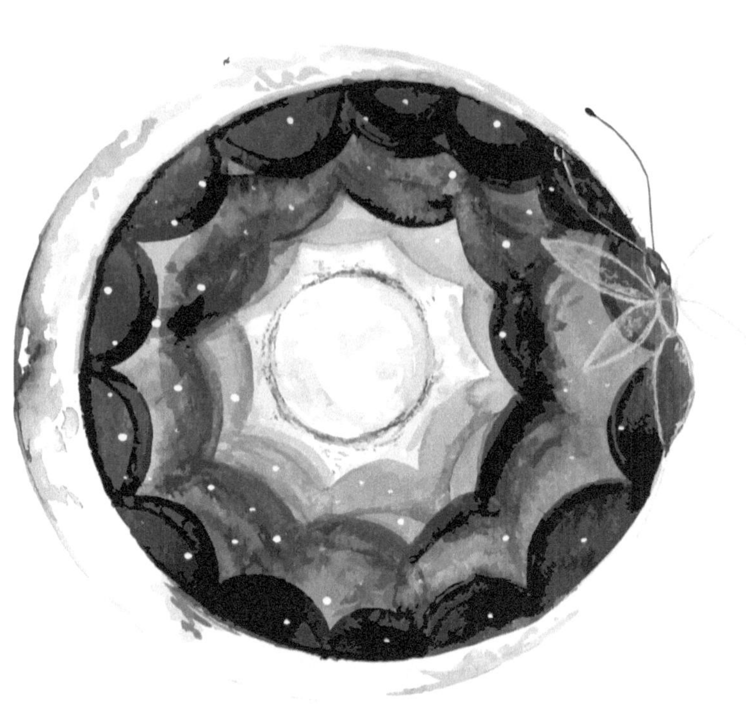

[o the dark places we will go]

o the dark places we will go
tiny violins & music from heavy
beaks will deafen in black
penetralia on wings of a black
fly   heavenly prisms

angel skin plucked from green air

& o how the pulp bitters to ash
o regretful tongue in the temple
of oranges we call our own

white as the eyes when the color
they've been painted expires
& we wrap our teeth around the bruise

& eat the rot as our own

[azure orations
of the carnival gnome]

azure orations of the carnival gnome
sealed in the camel's pentagon:

the gypsy moth on the messenger's tailcoat
the coal eyestone by the peddler's shoe

the ouroboros rinsed in venom
[flickering] the shape of things unshaped

the coiled [oiled] parabola nest [wingspan]
the diamond creature cut in its square

the wayfarer's scrimshaw tokens
the ballad of the aphotic oyster

the magician rolling his barrel of whale oil
to the copper furnace

the strangler fig playing its vermilion fiddle
to the plover   arrowed in wild substance [feral]

the snakestone cobwebbed in hexagon's fable
[storytelling]   bedfellow to the regalia

the kaleidoscopic walnut reddening
the cicada burrowed in buttongrass

the scarecrow's vestment
& the farmer's torch

the comet spewing its loneliness
the intoned ornament's mute quiver

the marionette in the porcelain canoe
the fleshlike paragon of idleness

[a thin ticket to a lightless city]

a thin ticket to a lightless city

idle in prayer   suddens the iris

     an arrow spins a drop of blood

     a fishwife tiptoes on cobblestone

here   the dark lantern leans against no rock

     a clocklike shift exposes the wax

     cubed in the teeth of a goblin's grin

silvered on a naked bell

black-footed & olive

     its crossbones glowworms

     its feet tealeaves

tapping the notes of a splintered flute:

a hymn as we carry our baskets of mice

[in the shade of a
star-drunk cherry tree]

in the shade of a star-drunk cherry tree
a swan hangs mute from a godless jaw

pine needles on black water fan amber
invocations   tremble an acorn

on the red lion's spine
the north star falls   bitters the lion's breast

pulls from its life what death can't steal
a blackbird alights on the horn of a ram

breaks rain from icy bone
bedews a young clover in a white seashell

below: no flower stays in bloom

[skull: skin-covered castle]

skull: skin-covered castle

cherry-pale nest mothering

shell-less yolk

dipped in thieving sun

the glass-bottom house

a witness to lilac roots

or us [with clean mouths]

standing on hooks

[in triduum he washes
his hands with secondhand]

in triduum he washes his hands with secondhand

soap & as the soap shrinks small bones appear

he waits & cleans the unshelled remnants

at noontide   & orients the sphinxlike fractals

into an hearted masterpiece: a totem

in galvanized solstice [the third day: inklike]

& with clean hands he splays the humid phenomenon

into icebergs   thawing schism palmed   & gone

[hands which once held the darkening]

hands which once held the darkening

flower of when now wed in nude time

skin shared with watery dream

held close by the breath

of a god-nourished hour

a honeyed embrace on the breast

of once & what's to come & once

there were children here

once there was moon & we chose our fruit

& wings are what hands wished to be

pure yellow hearts & ours were once here

locked slowly in clean-curtained rooms

[i spin the flower
with three fingers]

i spin the flower with three fingers
& [unhinge] there are no soft hours
no silken moments
only that which is always breaking

[something is always
breaking here]
& left only with middle

i know why the wish-tick assumes

[o the dark places we will go]

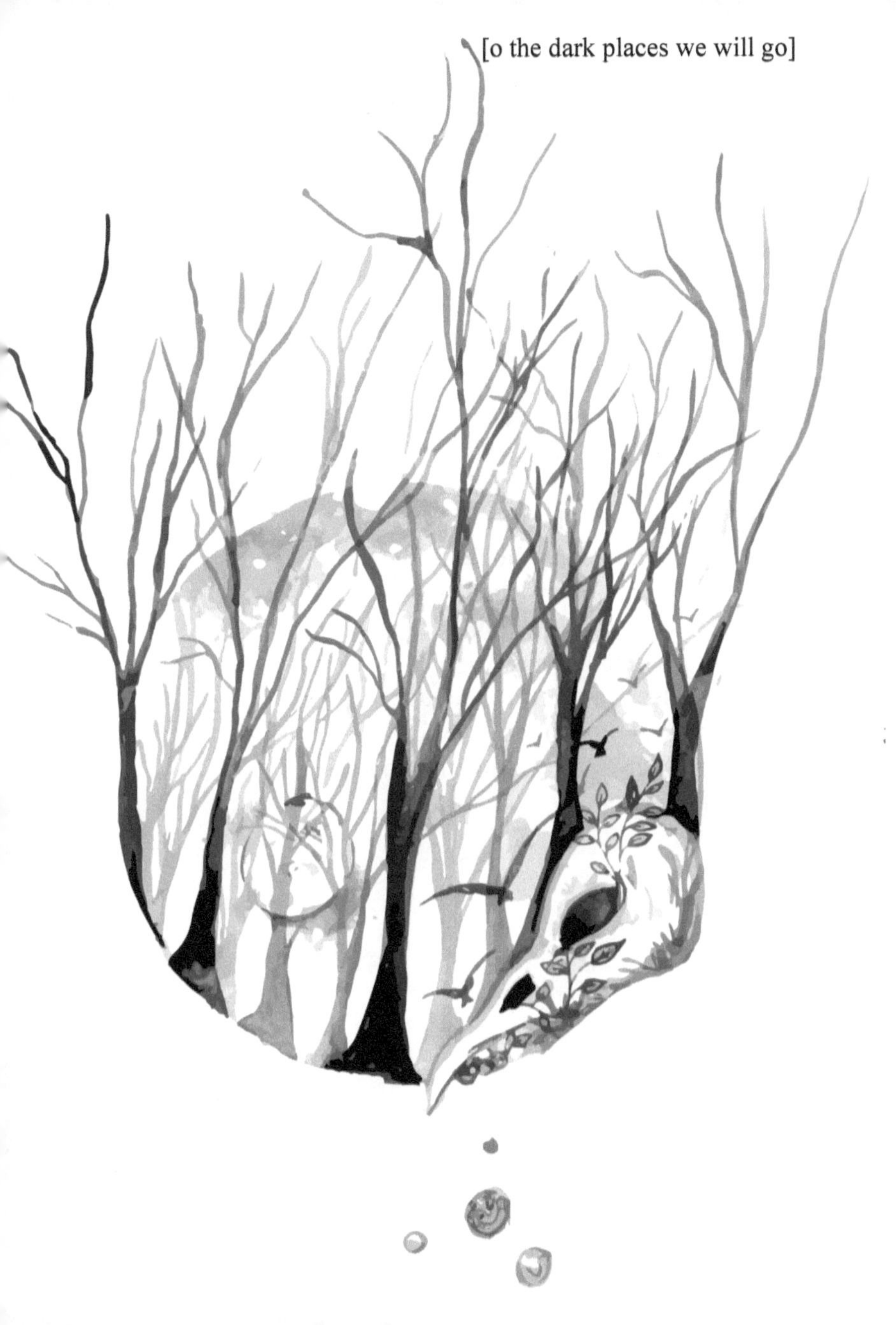

[my fingers   damp
in a ruined dream]

my fingers   damp in a ruined dream
hold tiny mirrors to her ashen face
eyes   caught like two scant fish
cast back   by tears that failed to see
themselves before the sad   her fingers
exhume vellum word-coffins
from pockets no hands should find:
starless reveries of a prophet's dusk
confessions of crimson   blue   asters
on bones   painted bones
[morts graines d'amour] & the rude
beauty whispers: plant the bones
know they'll grow to become the flowers
ours will never be

[there is a puppet in the grass who wants to eat]

there is a puppet in the grass who wants to eat

the clover but can't because it has no mouth

but it can taste the sulfur in the rain & it does

not make excuses for the hermetic jackrabbit

who pulls at the string of lights around its waist

in the hope of climbing to the sun when the sun

can't climb that far when the moon is tongueless

& cannot vow to the monks that the black seed

in her heart is really a diamond or how she shone

on the orange cats who threw dice

because the puppet is the fifth paw the tongue

that wants to lick but can't & glued to the agate's

nexus hope like blue fish in hot honey

[her bones found] there are no flutes in this

red moss kingdom no wintry plums or wormwood

tea only the farthest vessel moored in dream

so it lets tantric teeth feast on the crystals stitched

to its skin: i will not join them by eyelock i crush

the brow bones & paste a new mask to my face skin

& as i hold my egg to the light i hear the crumbs

of a peripatetic gargoyle jingle in my eardrum & i

wonder how long the thing inside has been frozen

like the gargoyle meant to forever look down

i don't know how to rebuild the fires of yesterday

from the ash i'm left wiping from my hands

or how to feed it but i do

[white pebble levitates in black ice]

white pebble levitates in black ice

an eye to watch the red house
that lives on its side

[scarlet mandala
devoured in equinox]

scarlet mandala devoured in equinox
withdraws into its nightshade tangle
& absorbs [absolves] its berries:
i think of how chance paired us
like trumpets & wicks [unpinned]
left to seek maps on heartwood
to the places you bottled your herbs
& preserved your rosewater tinctures
tubed chemical potions: magnetic
precipitations now spiderwebbed
in the cabinet   & like worldly things
[lace & pewter] idle elements calcify:
coral floats up the staircase   the urn
ajar on its storey   omnipotent
instruments left to polish while god
collapses uncolored   [our] onyx void

[the white bat creeps under the brick]

the white bat creeps under the brick

as valiant rain drubs leaves on descent

soaks trunks with muddy spatters

like the painter doesn't care

& you   dripping with liquid moon

dancing to the smoke

of a thousand burning silks

glued to sparked air

in a soliloquy of black paper roses

a cup full of tongues crossing their legs

[the firefly during the day
is just another bug]

the firefly during the day is just another bug
in gravity's bioluminescent night-cube of air

the color of evolution & instinct to survive
a reminder of nature's neon yellow circuit

dead stars give way to newborn light
as the moon unhooks powdery cloud

every color releases energy into things alive

& i think of how light is nothing except
a black exoskeleton with two wings & a head

[when i fall into white a bell rings]

when i fall into white a bell rings

in the hand of a wooden god an angel

plucks silvery threads of a lyre

& truth thaws

lightning flakes my skin [inward]

& i know the skylark's offing heart

i know the omen:

it's not a good thing

it's not what a thawing thing looks like

when an ivory prayer melts on the tongue

like a verse burning in red water

[nine serpents writhe in sleep]

nine serpents writhe in sleep

charms at a devil's cotillion

runes carved in blue clay

under nine bellies illume

secrets to the skinless moon

ivory crow caws

white magic gods fall

from coral cirrus bodiless

feathers float in hot ether

one river blood-silver [energy]

red seahorses flame in gold water

two saguaros cross spines

the hour wasp awakens

[o the dark places we will go]

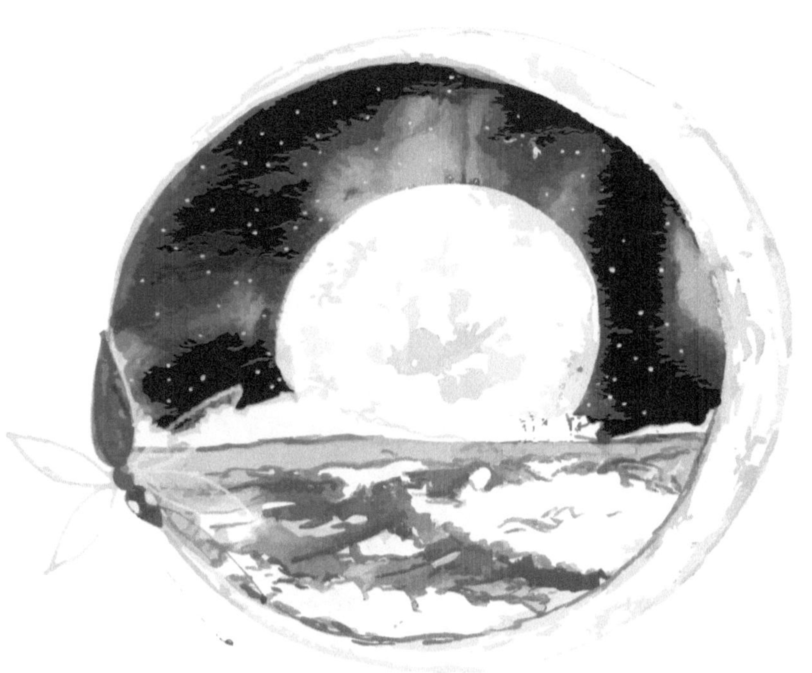

[o the dark places we will go]

The Hour Wasp

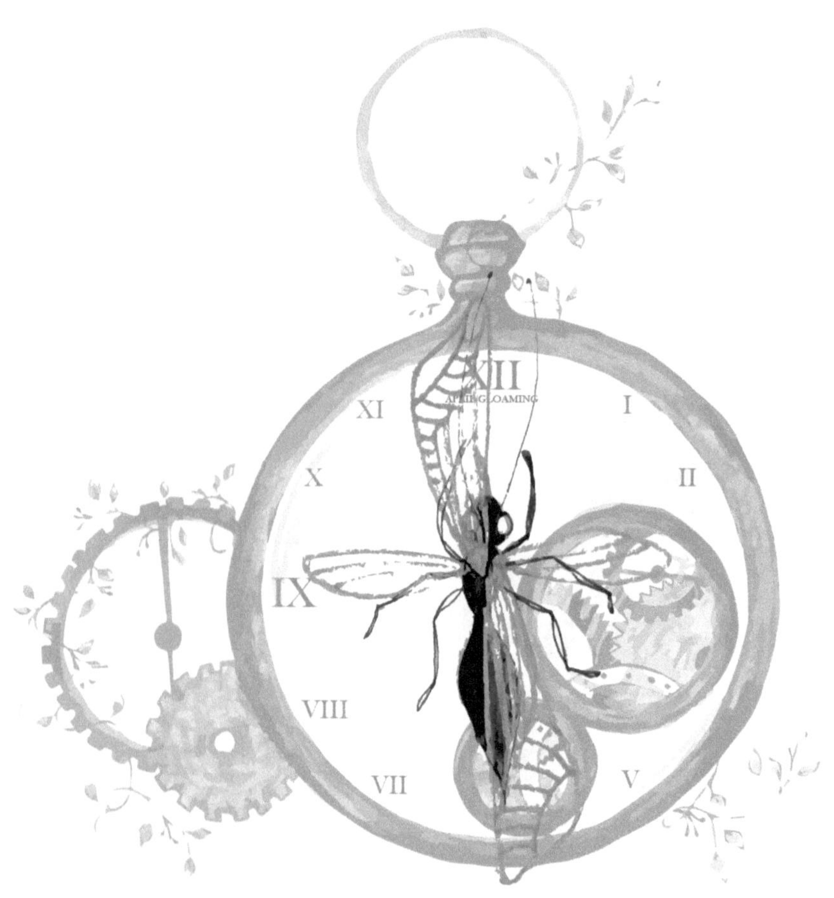

II

[blue haunts black]

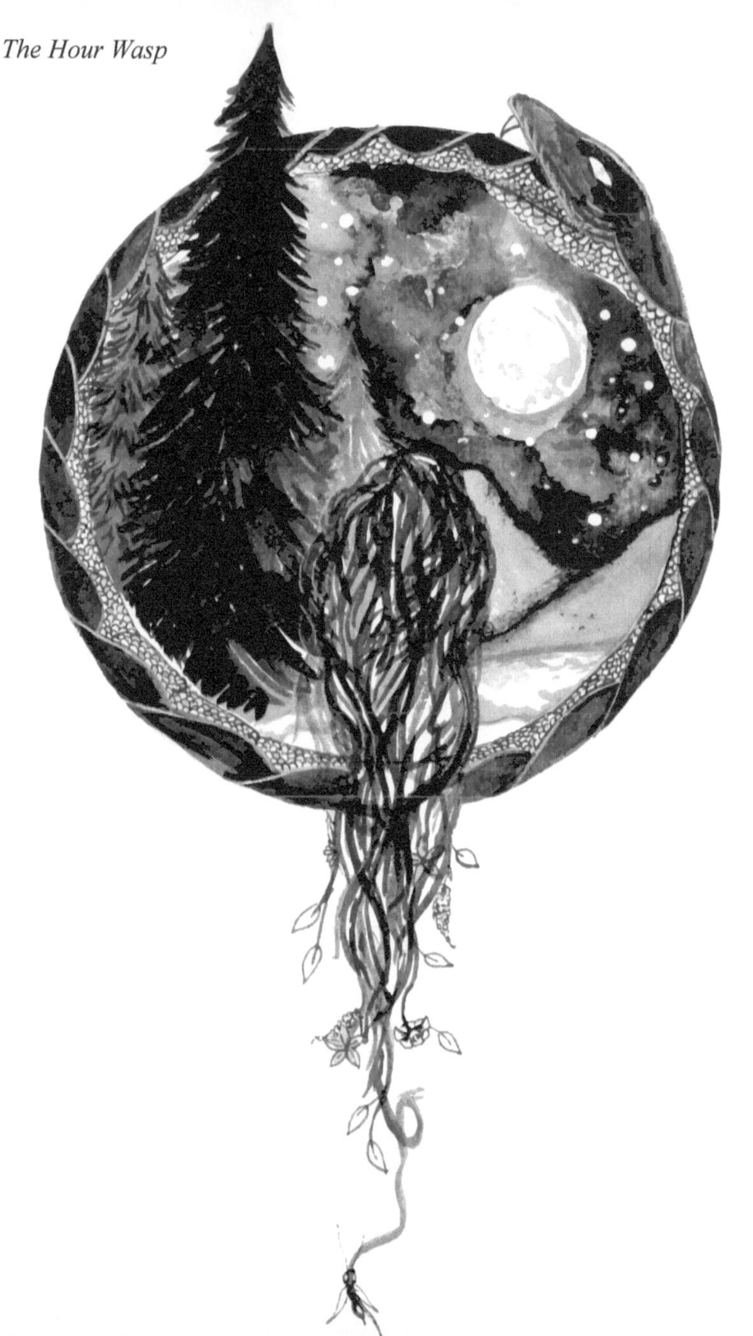

[blue haunts black
& i know you when]

blue haunts black & i know you when

i roam the foothills of our youth birdlike

& eat the bread from our clay pot of thorns [unmedicined]

& you & i in divine dark hatch white in the belly

as shine breaks open: the fire-horse in the frostless field

& [orbs]   the light

& we are the things that take shape

& we let the things without shape take shape

as the birds turn into coins

& then music the darkling fugue [the salted nocturne]

& the black wind crumbles

& still we wear those halcyon crowns   somewhere

[i drop a rosary of seeds]

i drop a rosary of seeds

i catch a tiny fish

i dig through pearled belly

i pillage the bones

i place flesh on unbloodied stone

i drink the light of a cold blue star

i set my wings aflame

i know my blood

there is no sin here

it has yet to be written

i cut my name on seashells

white with flowery throats

i sing from where all good things sleep

i eclipse skylike & drink my stones

did the moon ever look at our

blue-quartz eden & wonder

[a quickening heliolatry darkened]

a quickening heliolatry darkened
an oneiric chaos [fata morgana]
pure

a bent halo in tune
an epicedium of a dead seed
the psalm of a dying star

red serpents cross glass tongues
the riddle of the one-winged swan
all the days know when to sleep

the ten moons of etz hachayim
night's purpling sphere:
a continuum on time's
third hand wrinkled in pulse
the map of an opulent world

a hermit dismantles saturnian charms
by an empty river
breaks bread with a lemon-colored turtle
belly-up
[paper for the bloodless beast]

tiny daemons sail on white clay
a thousand suns unbutton
plum-colored sky
a wishbone in seawater
deaf as teeth

time: the long man who fades into stone
holds black ivy prayer

eternity: a blue nest of gold leaves
aflame in the light of the once-was

tadpoles hatch in the bottom-fire
a telestic lamp
cerulean: a holy color   wet
the seventh lotus sinks

a cathedral of splintered mushrooms [collect]
a pear rots on steps stained with obedience

the gatherer
the elephant & the blind man
unfold
into hundred-handed light

god: a large metal cube on sand
rinsed in milk   a place of finding
the river that flows four ways

[baby owl with a broken leg]

baby owl with a broken leg

limps into a motherless cage

ties itself back together

with red ribbon

sips used light

from prayer's green glass

[a caterpillar curls
on a heart-shaped whalebone]

a caterpillar curls on a heart-shaped whalebone

on shore a black branch casts its amber resin spell

on wanting soil: the witching tree

roots spit ruby pennies on a hemlock's toeprint

hooves & hanging grapes wear yellow

crystal skin [seaspray] in grass nearby

a bluestem grasshopper meditates with shiva lingam

prays to the peacock with its beak sewn shut

the sea & the never-moth: melancholy & buried

in a feathery blue box: the hope for better earth

[earthworm king frees its skin]

earthworm king frees its skin

the vapor lantern

a table of souls pinch rock salt

[blue haunts black]

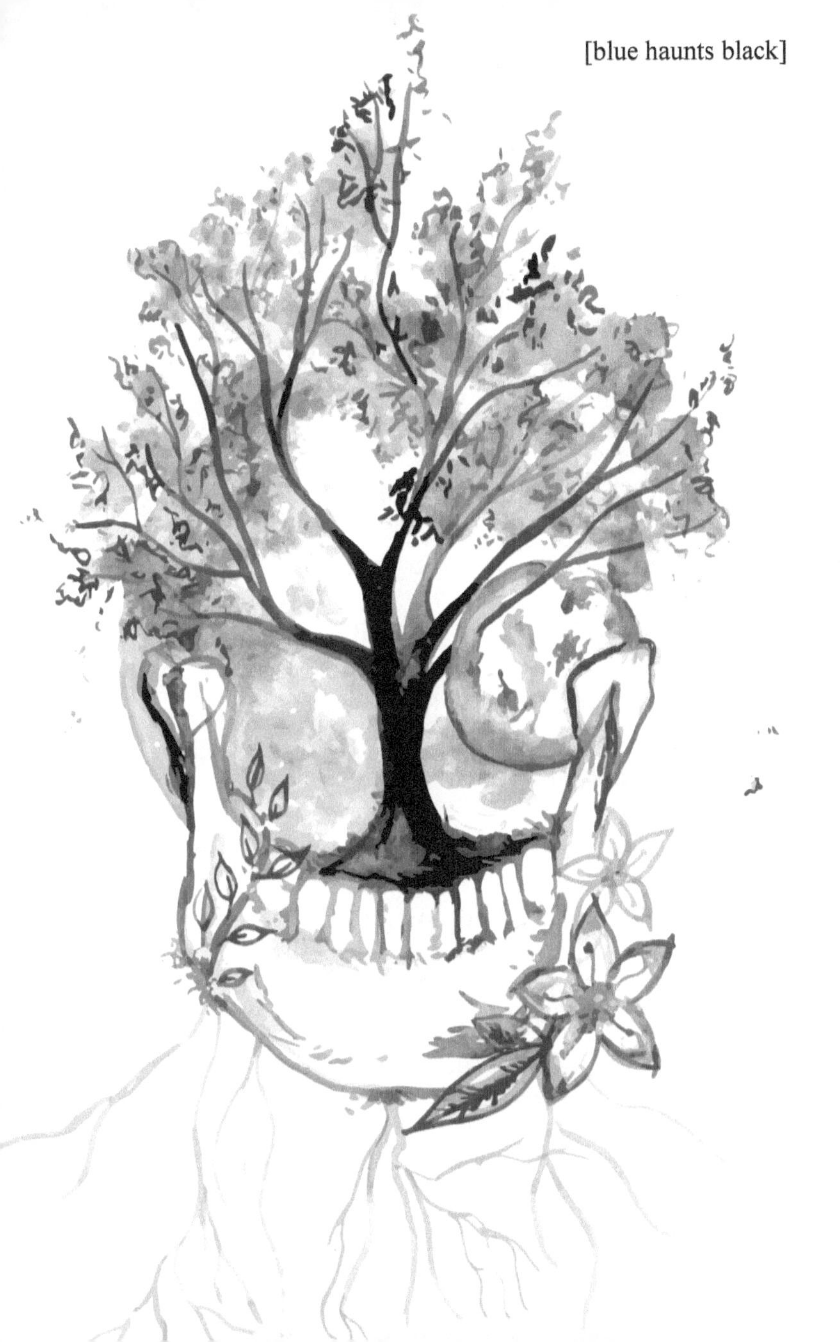

[hours stick & the ripe ripens
rot twice to brown]

hours stick & the ripe ripens rot twice to brown

this sober pareidolia in blue ink to be poked

with nervous sticks [red eyes] & this is where poet

becomes product of pinecones & gunmetal

& holy-glassed words: our thorn-on-thorn or graphic

sacraments to melt on the ribs like a verse in heat

where the symbol is magnified [cubes & cups]

to drink from where dark things wander: evaporation

in the pregnant room   quickening like the raven

to the shrew   when magic bleeds the god-awful spoon

[the grapevine swallows its statues]

the grapevine swallows its statues

& half the night

she watches a beak

pull meat from a zealot's grave

where an inchworm borders a time

when ears could be touched by sound

she strings her locket to a peppertree

& waters her starfield

neptune turns on its side & roams the edge

& time touches eggshell

& a salamander cherries its starlore

she whispers a wish

to the praying mantis frozen on spidersilk

whispers something about the starlings

& how their limbs turn to gypsum when they bleed

she is a desert rose   a wildfire

[the nomad unearths
a papyrus tetrahedron]

the nomad unearths a papyrus tetrahedron

from malefic silt [alluvial wasteland]

places it in his ninth pocket

steals a burnished saucer from his healer's satchel

sends buckled prayers to seventy-two directions

unstones a noble pebble from its roots

purges the rogue seed [heavy ore] twice

& ciphered through myth's crimson pigment

[unstirred] the aporetic descendant's antidote

[there's a secret in the pygg jar]

there's a secret in the pygg jar

in the residuum smudge of the keeper's dome:

the pygg's eyes are punched through clay

they've seen the snailshell float in the birdbath

& the piranha perish in sunken firmament

after they pried moongaze from the peeping conch

they've seen the castle of cocoons spawn bitter

crinkled steles at vishnu's bazaar

they shed three tears

when leather sandals floated across christ's water

the candle blinks a lavish ache

the white dog in the corn still knows atlantis

[o the joy in blue space]

o the joy in blue space
   & starbirds infused with night

the night   a cowardly thing
rounding the spheres of sunken nests
   & dewey-eyed toads
thumbing their way to the pond's edge
never to know the weight
of a magpie's stare: a glimmer
& all the saints kneel to their lips

a kiss on cold forehead

[tomorrow has already
wept its tears]

tomorrow has already wept its tears as father crow

blackfire brother ignite dandelion seeds in her heart

a pendulum aflame in the quickening tower of aevum

two suns cup the burning tree [a ghost-wish]

liquescent roses of release drip & luck is the spoon

bowled & burned from the heavy branch of need

a hermetic chrysalis of grievances opened like a casket

by memory's hand [oil & coin but no shine]

church bells & the sky ring blue breaths of mercy

rising to her planet's yellow-minted roof

silver pitchforks & tiny lanterns scratch shadows

on holy glass while moon swims through milky jars

copper winter-clock   no hands burnt hands

hold damp purple flowers like an epoch in burst

a bent wheel on the carriage sounds morning

& the little girl places her note in the box: in the interior

words have to let go   they have to let go to say so

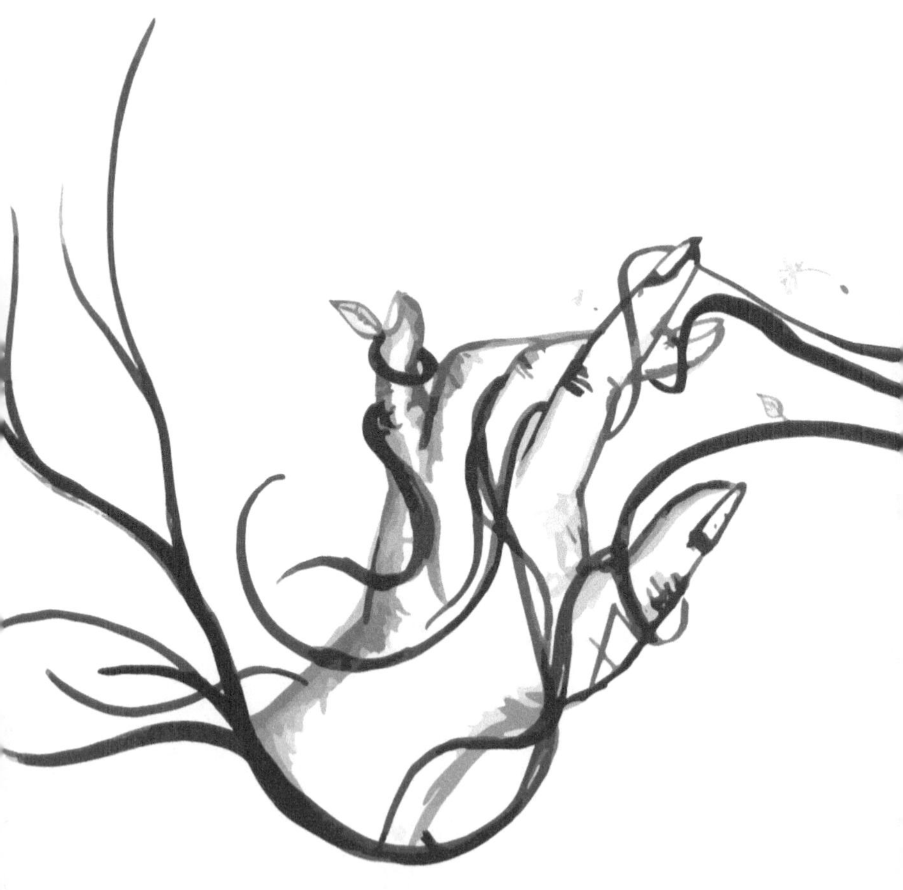

[blue haunts black]

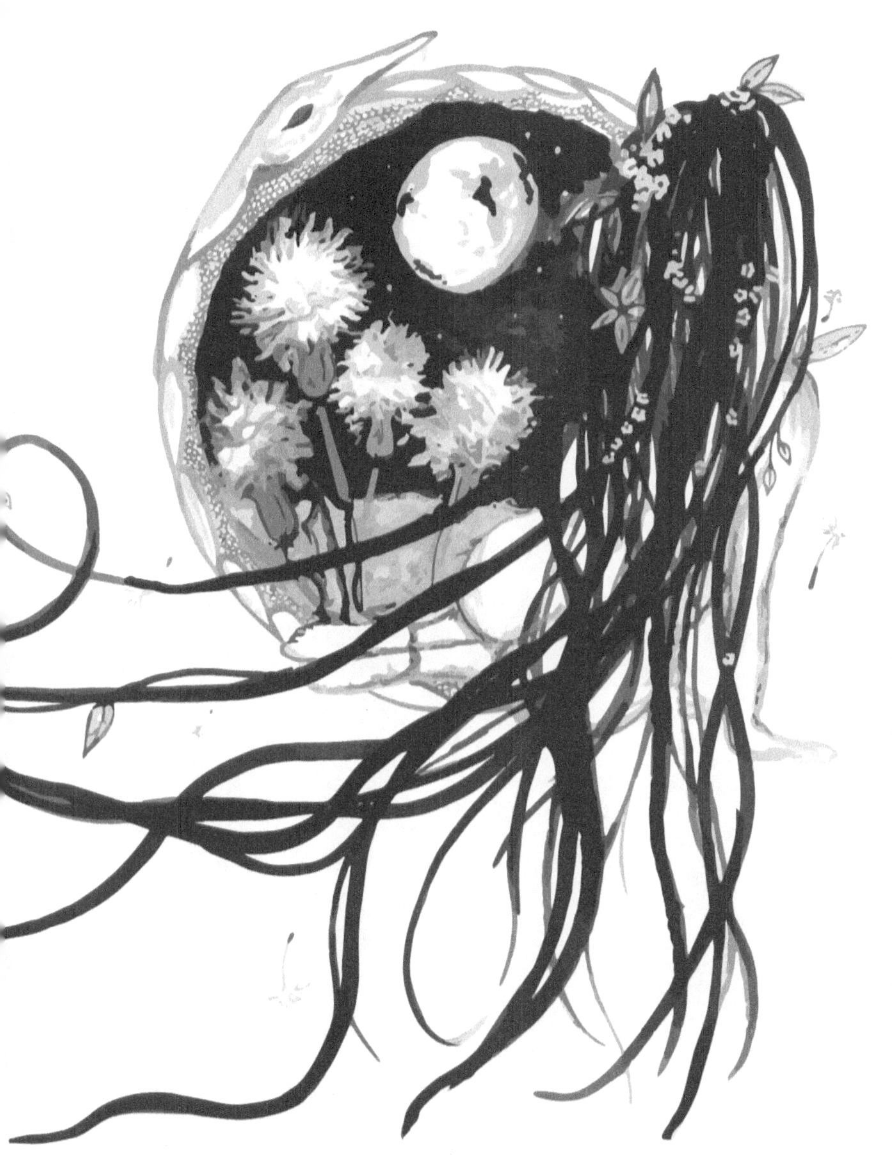

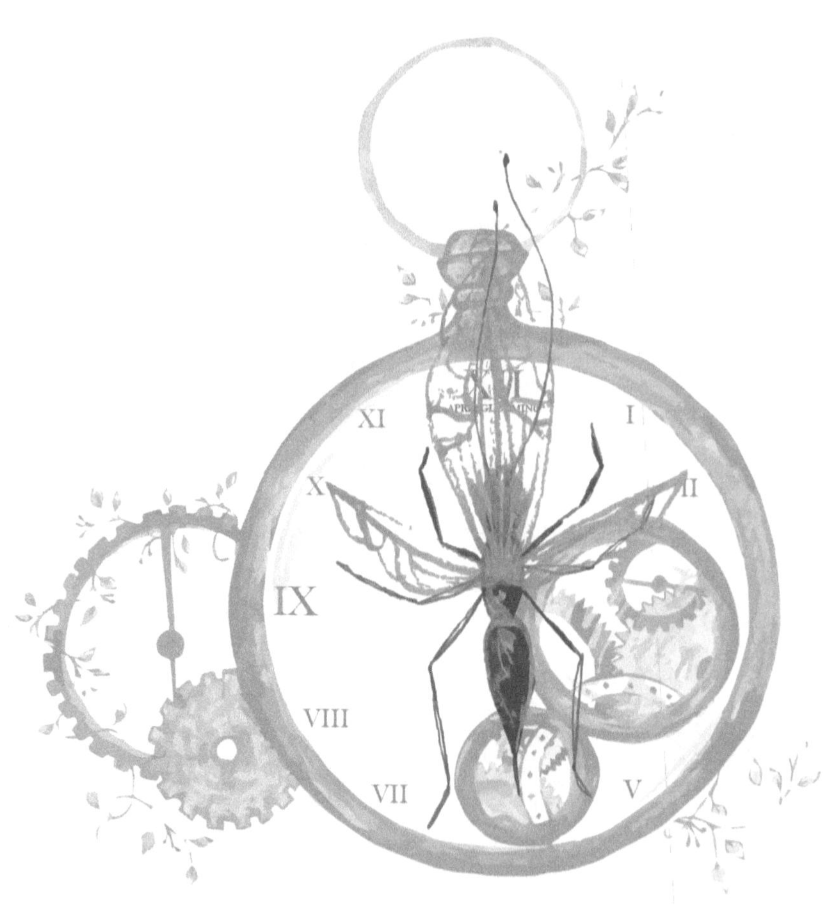

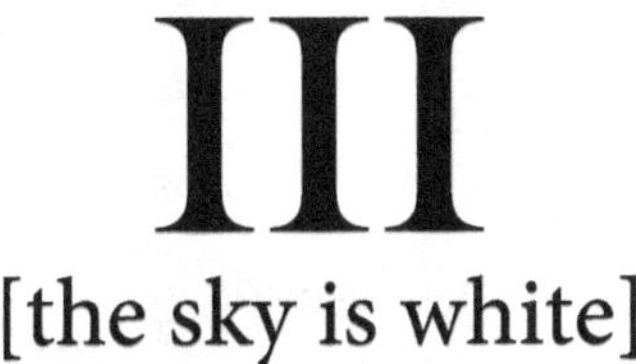

III
[the sky is white]

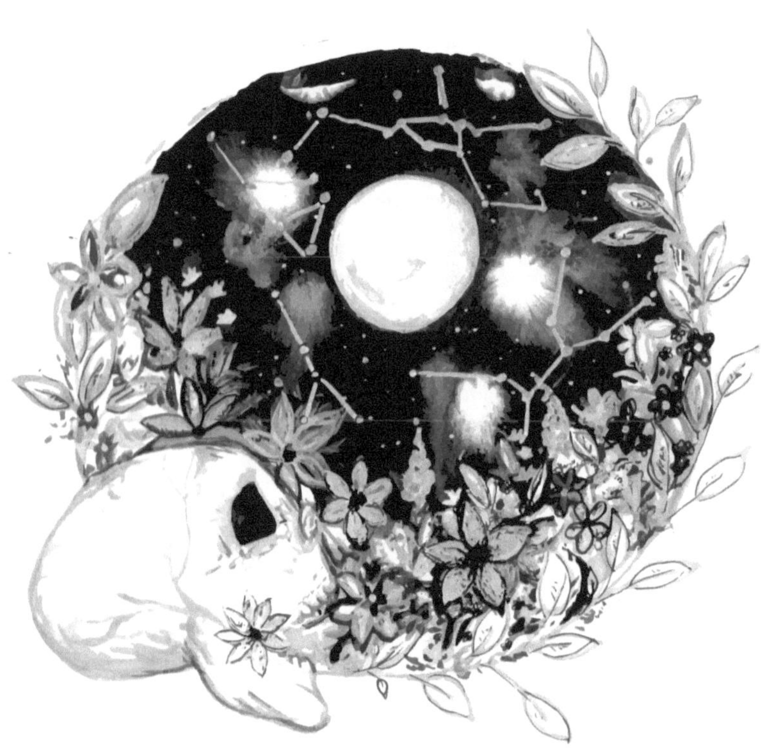

[the sky is white from the heat
of the lion licking the axe]

the sky is white from the heat of the lion licking the axe

a meridian of eyes on the butterfly's wings go blind

we dream ourselves snake tongues & drum wet rock

with song   black tusks wear us in glossolalia

sheltered in the circle of a central fire

the moon the child of god resurrected nightly

heaven's jawbone: whiter than snowmelt

cricketsong mirrors the void

ghostprint names spill from our throats

gold pinecones split open: the story

of how the beast lost its teeth in a field of triangles

[i hugged myself as a child & told]

i hugged myself as a child & told

myself that everything was perfect in the petrichor

the smell of pure innocence & earth & earthly

innocence that stays in the clothes i only wear

on good days [yellow threadbare]

i told myself that i'd chosen my world

that i'd chosen   my god

that i'd chosen the ones who'd leave all too soon

& i told myself that there were nine ponds

& that i'd walk on each one: each one a hard color

one: an azure crescent [borrowed light]

& that there'd be frogs & all things quick

& that i'd dig a key from the sand by the owl's foot

after the hourglass turns to smoke

& time calls my hands to dig & i'm there

by the ninth pond wondering

about the freewire son & the space within three

& jacob's other ladder

rising from the canyon like a pearl never found

or a pearl found that becomes moon

& i grow into the moon

& tie a red string around my wrist [orbit]

[born from the garden
grown of gold in a black robe]

born from the garden grown of gold in a black robe

he walks into a world possessed by new light unlocked

he breathes upon his lips a suprahuman slake

for cold pink-petaled water   to drink the gods down

to evaporate into plumed pareidolia a milk-feathered thirst

sunflowers bend & drop seeds: salt time with purpose

while fragrant sins forgive the moon as the sun

paints white on the bone   a ribcage

spun with webs clings to the belly of a bridge

over royal water [an emblem of holy power]

a hierophany from the huntsman's thread

five moths [powdery touchstones] crown

a rusted spike with an eye chalked fresh on the head

he arrives at a burnt iron door where a child

holds a yellow umbrella   frosts the word pearl

in white breath on red stones   the great world folds

[i pour the edge of my earth
from an empty cup]

i pour the edge of my earth from an empty cup
i sit with myself as an old man
we are in the desert   i am older   i am old
& we hold our empty cups like the leaf holds water

& like the leaf i turn over & give myself to the roots
the roots whisper to catch the crying opossum by its tail
to pull the earthbound map from its back
& write a windsong to the curious bowl of flesh:

how it looks like the head of an unwinged body who hides rain
& this is why we have deathbeds
why we spin our stones into sphered cacophonies

in the desert: i listened to my life as it silenced me

[her black hair shines
among the evergreens]

her black hair shines among the evergreens

she is sitting on a wooden bench under starlit sky

she calls me forth silently

i sit beside her

& tie my breath to her body

i see the thousandth star

she looks to the thousandth star

the thousandth star is us

& the sky empties into a peppered blue flame

[the sky turns to smoke
as if to say i'm guiltless]

the sky turns to smoke as if to say i'm guiltless

a black tree cloaked in lichen stares fresh from the womb

watery bone obeys mute moon: the illusory choir

the night-queen's beehive & all her children work footless

i leave my other home & pray earthlike

[emerald bulbs hang in atziluth]

emerald bulbs hang in atziluth
a noetic greenness [initiatory]

under gossamer-jeweled selva
the numinous white-eyed panther:

a knowing   the seeker
in the monk's civara [clockwise]

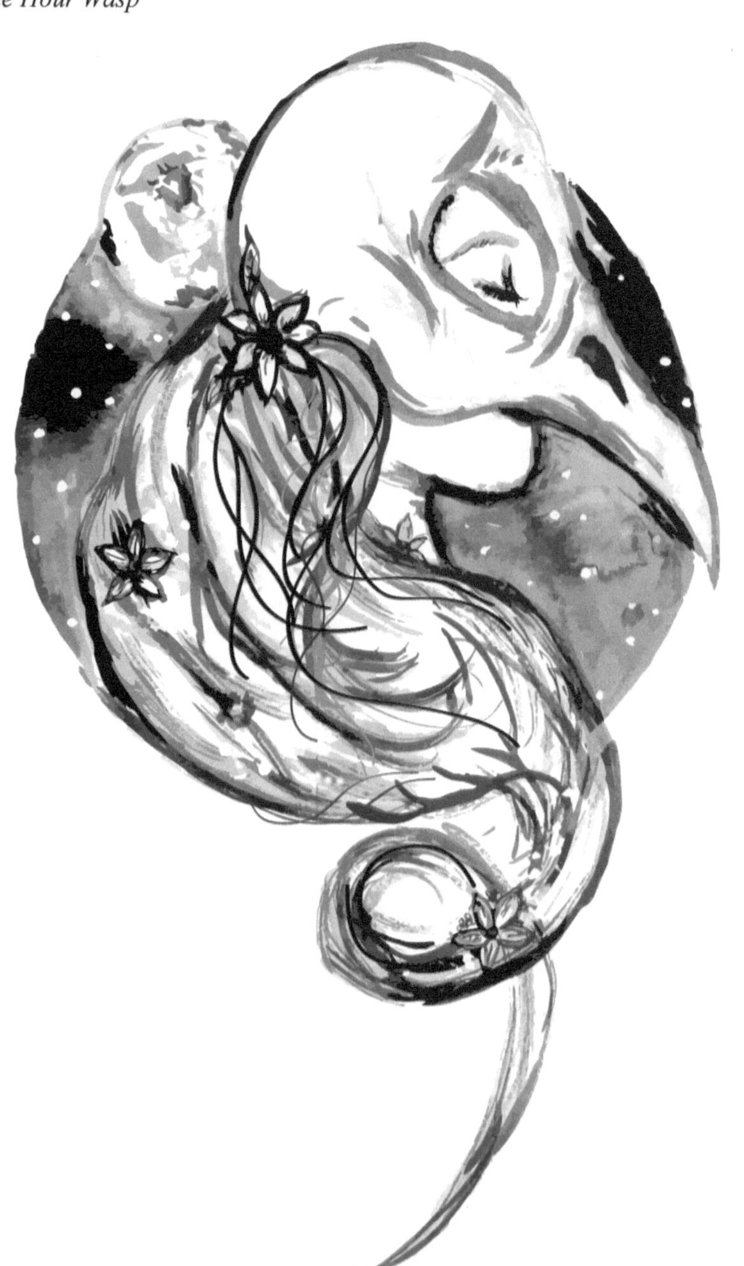

[the moon exists]

the moon exists
& we're an art

a word throat-locked
to kiss on the world

horsemen who hold
our belongings in roses

[starfired sphinx
half in the belly choked]

starfired sphinx half in the belly choked

a golden bush in fog reveals its treasure
to the rabbit in pinkening ascent

three books rest under earthlight
as a pearl melts under the gum tree

an orange moth flutters [luminous]
on the dead goose's throne

a needle disappears when held to the sun

a nautilus carries its former lives in walled-off rooms
behind itself: unnamed roots of a stelliferous life

there's a reason why spiders wear teeth on their legs

starshine in a hole in the middle of a gray stone is home
to a purple plant: a heart beating in gradations

the argonaut floats toward other worlds while satellites
mistaken for stars tell how our heavens are littered

i walk along the shore
& stop only for stones that look like kneecaps:

two white trees drop their swords
as i pull the bee from my mouth

[in burnt-ivory morning air
an ensouled plume inks]

in burnt-ivory morning air an ensouled plume inks

the sky from the chimney of a stone crematory

on a hill in the woods   once a fragile container

of memories to come   now an obsidian crest

to the knowable world: a lumpy decanted moment

how time appears as change appears

in my mind tucked safe i think i will not

be this augury to a future poet   no

i'll be a sapphire vessel transcending the sense-world

that only exists because it once was versed

once was imaged like a tortoise shell full of proverbs

or foxglove in orange-vanilla nightfall

myself   a black ox perhaps   awakened to every

thing   awakened to how a gull feather folds over to white

on a foamy shore as a hermeneutic fish chokes

while no one is watching   or maybe

i'm a stitcher of olive branches   a magician

with a nightingale on a string of knots & a lover's

perfumed linen note tucked square in a handsewn pocket

who ponders why as we age we rinse our straw clean

i imagine this smoke   once a man or woman

or child even   with dimples   & watch

as he she or the little one touches the dawn high

as snowflakes poke through the sooty vestige

of what it means to be human & i wonder if i

or anyone i know   should be so lucky & i light

a new fire at the end of myself

[the hermit triples
wet light by four:]

the hermit triples wet light by four:
a coronation [unegged]

he undrinks the hailstone
a spiral slice sevens the eyelid

a fish eye in the sparkling jaw
& the ever-burning oath eats its god godlike

[the poet leapt into
the cavern   fiddled]

the poet leapt into the cavern   fiddled

with some rocks that looked like bees:

the queen turned her head

      in history it was snowing

a fingernail was stuck to a wall of feathery clay

the poet looked at his hands & thought of thirst

how thought is thirst

& pondered a riddle of wine & ring

[…]   all things all things all things are

      predictions   the poet

leapt into the cavern to forge a samurai's signature

on a blood orange [proper] to lament his green pages

[to explore beauty]

to explore beauty
is to implore forgiveness from an emptiness

only beauty can fill

[may her words be ruins
nude on sand]

may her words be ruins nude on sand
for he who wanders heart in hand

talons disguised as voices pierce your third eye
you step carefully into yourself
they steal your skin   slice through hushed
pain: you are supposed to know that you bleed
as your brothers do

they prey on heavy bone   beg you to seek delicacy
in the ash of what it means to be human as they dig
          lucid as the liquid self
drips like red honey from your roots

they rise from your flesh & become you:
encoded decoded an imagining a reimagining of a time
so cyclical you now know what it means to be both
the observer & the observed

the firsts   who under another sun died for you
& you now know why your feet have felt so heavy
[   ]: shiny & wet with good
power

the mystery is that you have forgotten the mystery
forgotten how you are words of the same riddle
written on sands of a landscape forever veiled by dunes
of past lives   the birds sing a hymn of ruin & heart
& profess: what time whispers is almost enough

they depart   raising a haloed sky off their wings

in this oasis of little birds a chipped arrowhead
gets tossed for another try as the hand of the breath-birther
writes history with the crack of a shell   a mimetic
desire to feed from what kills
[dark wings need no light for they are]
the sun dips: a decree that soon enough
it will be at your back now chasing
no longer the blazing compass
the iron in your blood begs to follow

the desert rises   the birds return to praise the crescent hand
& sew in the curtain of a red-dust night an empyreal
melody of the once great world:
the golden wander toward apples meant to rot
fruit on tongue   deaf to what is taught

centipede slips into smokestone   red petals furl
cold on the dune: the white air came too soon
you sleep a green-star slumber under a bell moon
crowned blue   saved on locked moss
time creates the middle breath & asks:
when the water thirsts   what does it thirst for

you follow the birds over hot dunes & settle unruined
into the sand beyond all sands
you see red ribbon   threads of gold
the lost hymns of cædmon for trade under mercury
music & flickering candlelight & a woman
hands you ambrosial water in an ivory cup
ghawazi dance to drums   songs
of the seven seers evaporate into the taste of night

sandalwood lingers   rope sinks into sand
a beggar is robbed of his bread
as thirteen dhows set sail toward aeolia

the oracles crush lapis clay & fishbone with pestle:
ink words to be kissed on the throat of a dove
bedouin tobacco   black opium
stars blink in the tamarisk
[fire scorch muscle salt teeth cut]
you're here but only she sees you

the woman reveals four patina snakes coddled
in cloth & breasts hungry for hoofbeats
swift earth   where silver foxes need not slaughter
[the prophetess of pearls] she tells you:
a pearl dropped in wine stains in mute time
& here you are a pearl   dropped in time
stained with what chokes you

she speaks of jinn   maps delicate songs
in their honor on her body in fire
no ink could stand   finger smokes over rim
an etheric nest   the mists are navigable   .

her henna-wrapped hand holds seven almonds:
spiced blackened dead stone fruit to break
on history's tongue   she hands you three
her lips lament: they never had wings
your skeleton fragile   the glass in her night
she bends a crown of nettle thorn & breathes:
there are no butterflies here

the scarabs rest   time is not visible but still
it rolls softly   swiftly   folding back into itself
like a heart on fire

you remember ezekiel's wheel was never a wheel
but an auric sky-body chariot blazing through thorns
like there was never a drought: a chokecherry dusk
pinned to armoured sea   you wake to thunder

the wind draws her last words on the sand
beside you: there once was a season so sacred

you stand knowing that in this world of perishable things
you are home   you walk where feathers
of birds fall   through fragments of your constellations

[i walk toward death's white forest]

i walk toward death's white forest

toward a yellow leaf stitched to a naked branch

when the wind takes me into a sky

beyond all skies

where wives & sons save final breaths

afresh by a celestial river of clear colors

& done taking

i am whispered into this world

to become who i'm to become

by the way of the breath-birther

[acknowledgements]

I am grateful to the editors of the journals *Hermeneutic Chaos*, *Aleola*, *Sundog Lit*, *Albion Review*, *The Light Ekphrastic*, *Enclave*, *Entropy*, *The Legendary*, *Apricity*, *Shot Glass*, *Black Elephant Lit*, and *The Poets' Touchstone*, where many of these poems appeared in earlier versions.

To the folks at Goddard College, who've witnessed and supported this work—thank you.

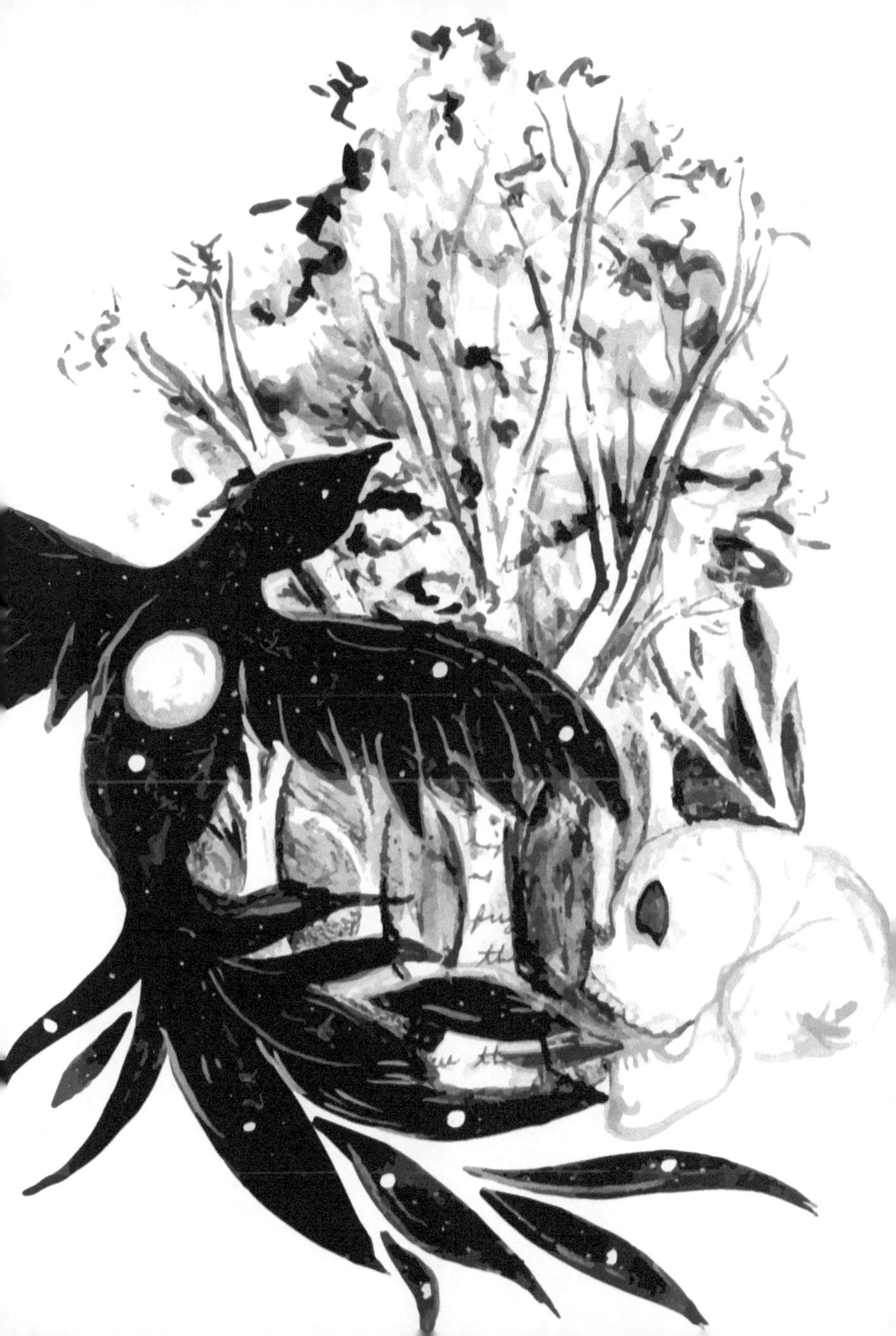

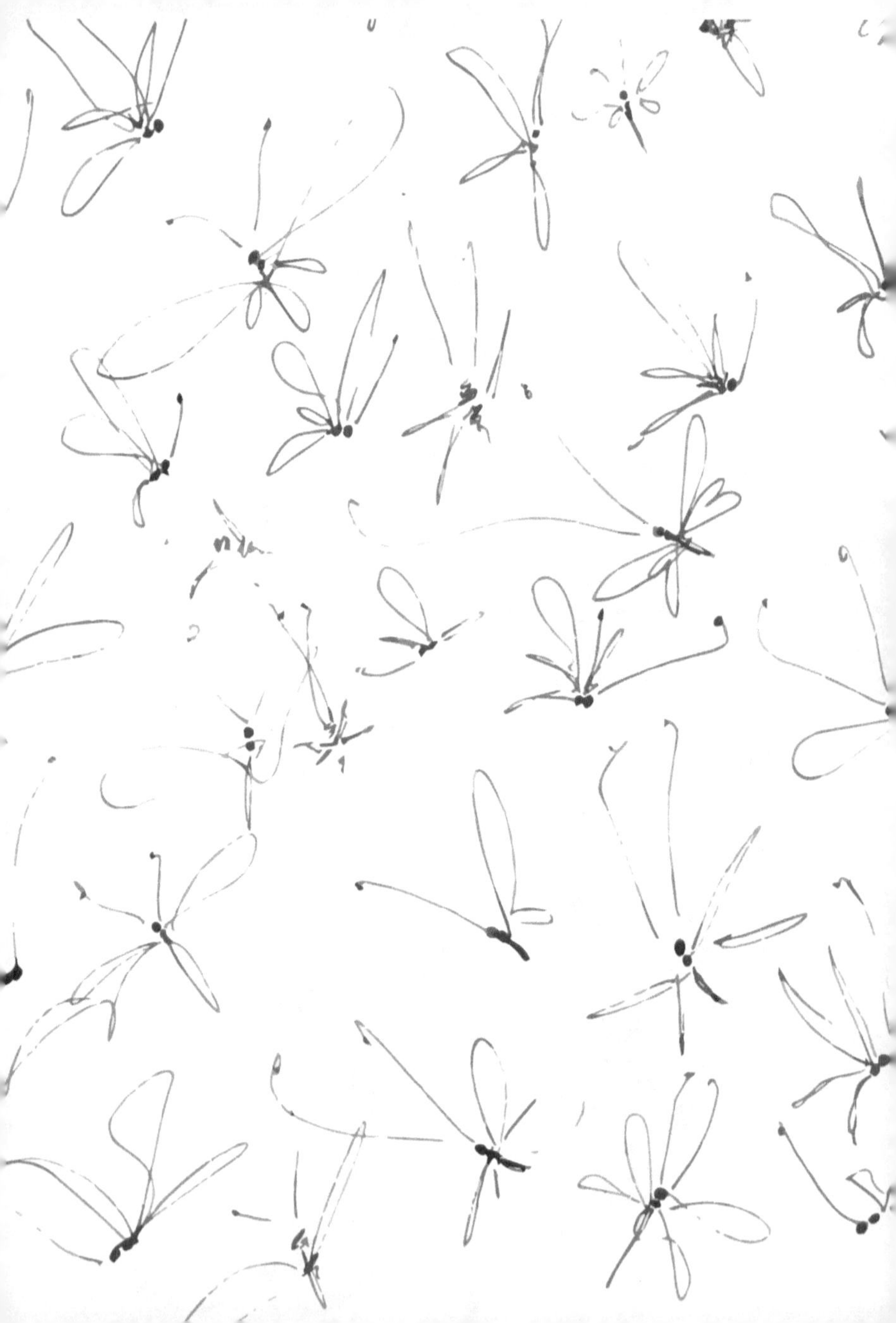

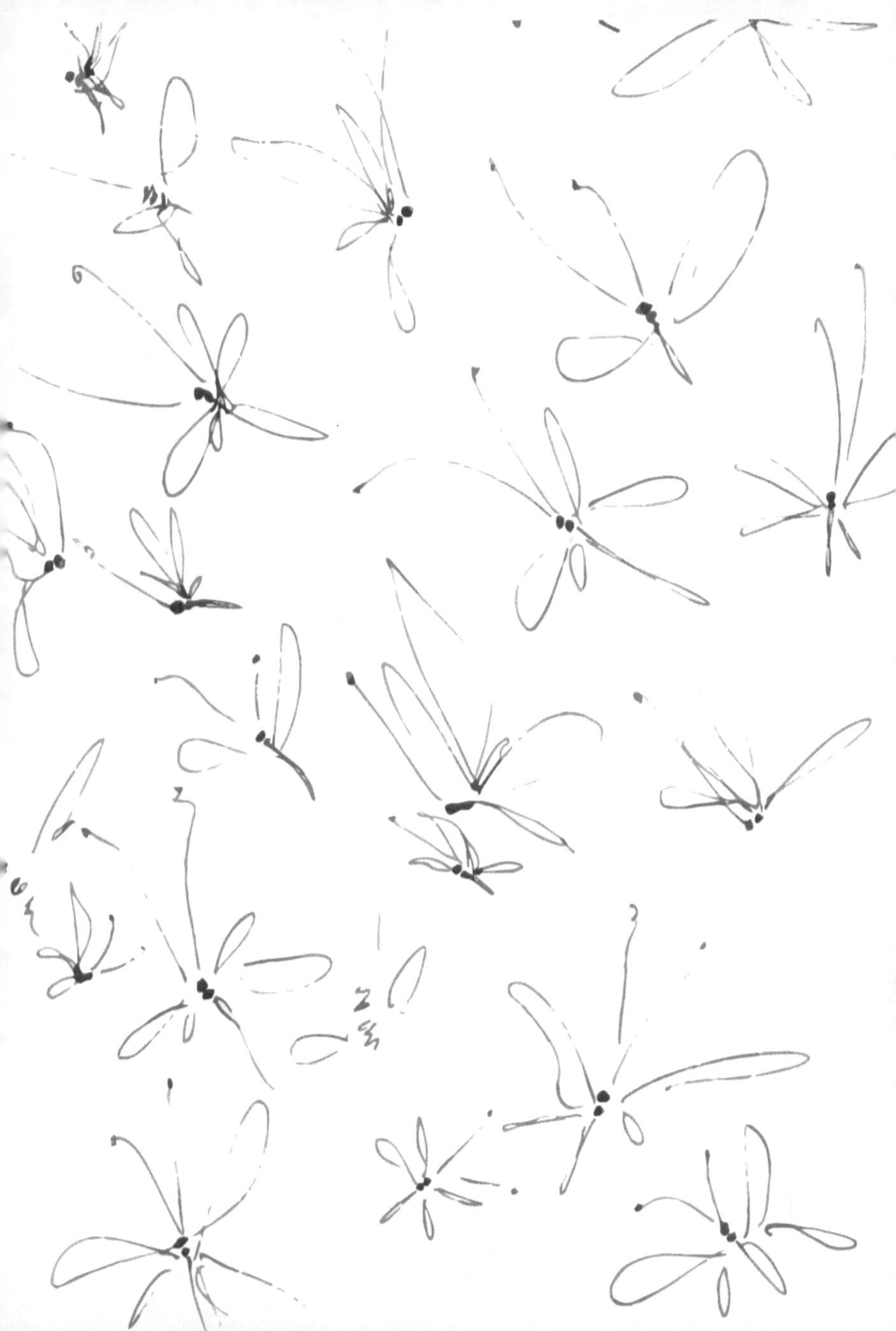